This delightful book is the latest in the series of Ladybird books which have been specially planned to help grown-ups with the world about them.

As in the other books in this series, the large clear script, the careful choice of words, the frequent repetition and the thoughtful matching of text with pictures all enable grown-ups to think they have taught themselves to cope. The subject of the book will greatly appeal to grown-ups.

Series 999

THE LADYBIRD
BOOKS FOR GROWN–UPS SERIES

BOXING DAY

by

J.A. HAZELEY, N.S.F.W. and J.P. MORRIS, O.M.G.

(Authors of 'I Can Make You Prime Minister')

Publishers: Ladybird Books Ltd., Loughborough
Printed in England. If wet, Italy.

There are two important days at Christmas.

There is Christmas Day, when everyone is jolly and hungry and very pleased to see each other.

And there is Boxing Day.

Jonathan and Oriane have gone for a Boxing Day walk with Transformers the dog.

Walking is healthy. It will help them digest their dinner.

And by the time they get home, Jonathan's father might have finished being racist and fallen asleep in his liquorice allsorts.

There is a James Bond film on the television. Debbie has been watching it for nearly an hour, but has not paid it much attention and cannot remember what has happened. Actually, it might be a Die Hard.

"I don't really like dates," says Debbie, as she starts another packet.

The inevitability of Trivial Pursuit is weighing heavily on Gaius and Napoleanne.

The box only comes out once a year, and the number of family members who can remember the medallists from the 1980 Moscow Olympics is dwindling.

Uncle Bernie weighed eight stone on Christmas Eve.

"I blame those pickled walnuts," he grumbles.

The first Boxing Day was the day after the baby Jesus was born.

Mary and Joseph were fed up with the mess and the braying and the constant stream of visitors, and kept tripping over piles of presents and just wanted some time on their own.

We re-create that magical day in our own homes every year, but with Lush bath bombs instead of myrrh.

The toilet door has been locked for hours.

The Viz annual is missing from the pile of books by the Christmas tree, as is cousin Brendan.

Eventually, the police are called.

Christmas is a good time to catch up with people you have not seen for a while.

Daphne and Delia have not seen the till staff at Debenhams for over 24 hours, so the Boxing Day sales have come just in time.

It said "non–drop" on the label attached to Polly's Christmas tree.

Yet, for the last week, she has had to hoover under it every few hours.

Her in–laws are arriving this morning, and Polly is thinking of telling them that it is not a tree, but an important sculpture making some point or other.

In this sewage plant, everyone has been busy preparing for the Boxing Day rush.

The sluices have been cleared, extra pumps installed, and all leave cancelled. They hope the equipment will be able to cope.

On the 27th, the exhausted and shell–shocked staff will head home to celebrate a belated Christmas with their families.

If Tasha has to sit through one more celebrity perfume advert, she will not be responsible for her actions.

Most of the puddings from yesterday have been finished, but there is still a trifle, a large jelly, a dozen éclairs, a raspberry Pavlova, a banana loaf, a treacle tart, a nut ring, a cranberry roulade, a chocolate log, two panettones, six boxes of mince pies and the Christmas cake.

And for afterwards, there is a nice refreshing Stilton.

This bauble came loose from the International Space Christmas Tree on Boxing Day 1996.

It has orbited the world every ninety minutes since.

The International Space Fairy, which is made of aluminium alloy coated with graphite fibre—reinforced epoxy and cost £600,000, is still in place.

Because Aunt Olivia has a dicky tummy, a runny nose, a habit of bursting into tears easily and a tendency to knock over her sherry, Gary wants to make sure he will not run out of toilet paper while the shops are shut.

So he has done a deal with a man down the docks.

Kevin is not really a Christmas person. He had put the tree out by the bins yesterday before the Queen had finished talking.

He scowls at it from the kitchen window.

"Those bin men aren't getting a tip from me. Other people work on Boxing Day," mutters Kevin as he fills in his V.A.T. return.

The crisp snow looks perfect for sledging, thinks Janet. She smiles at the thought of warm hats, cosy mittens, a walk, a snowball fight and a steaming mug of hot chocolate.

Sadly, the snow is not outside. It is in a photograph of what the family did last Easter.

Janet has been looking at old pictures on Facebook all day to take her mind off the Boxing Day drizzle.

Kelly has just remembered what she did with the overhead projector at the office Christmas party, so she is going to live in Bhutan for the rest of her life.

She will e—mail her resignation if they have e—mail at the convent.

The children received DVDs and video games for Christmas. They have been locked in Granny's spare room with the old television since Christmas morning.

Downstairs, the grown-ups can watch whatever they like on the big television.

There is nothing on but children's films.

"It's funny," says Chloe, "that all the presents fitted neatly under the tree, yet now they've been unwrapped, there is no room left in the whole house."

"I know," says Paul, from deep inside the mountain of cardboard, giftwrap and ribbons where he has been trapped since yesterday with nothing to eat except some Tia Maria.

The tip re-opens on January 6th.

Eddie usually spends Christmas commiserating with friends on social media who are also having trouble sleeping on a squeaking camp—bed under their parents' stairs, wrapped in a faded Thundercats duvet that smells like a wrestler's towel.

His phone ran out of battery this morning. No—one has a charger.

Eddie has taken up writing war poetry.

It is August, so these people are recording a television Christmas Special which will be shown on Boxing Day.

The studio is boiling hot. The presenter is not in the mood for eggnog. Melted brandy butter is dripping down his reindeer tie.

The presenter thinks Newsnight should not do a Christmas Special until they know what the news is, but television is very complicated.

Although Christmas decorations are not meant to come down until Twelfth Night, the council dismantles the tree in the market place at dawn on Boxing Day.

This marks the return of bus lanes and parking restrictions, while drivers are still too bloated and dozy to realise it is a Wednesday.

The fines will help pay for next year's tree.

This ship is carrying its regular post–Christmas cargo of 140,000 tonnes of those little plastic tags that attach toys to their packaging, so they can be buried in China as landfill.

The toys came from China. The tags go back to China.

Recycling is good for the planet.

Boxing Day officially ends in May, when this turns up in a tin on top of the fridge.

"Ah! I meant to get that out," says Mum, as she tips it into the brown bin.

And, finally, it is over.

THE AUTHORS would like to record their gratitude and offer their apologies to the many Ladybird artists whose luminous work formed the glorious wallpaper of countless childhoods. Revisiting it for this book as grown-ups has been a privilege.

MICHAEL JOSEPH

UK | USA | Canada | Ireland | Australia
India | New Zealand | South Africa

Michael Joseph is part of the Penguin Random House group of companies whose addresses can be found at global.penguinrandomhouse.com

First published 2016
001

Printed in Italy by L.E.G.O. S.p.A

A CIP catalogue record for this book is available from the British Library

ISBN: 978-0-718-18486-5

www.greenpenguin.co.uk